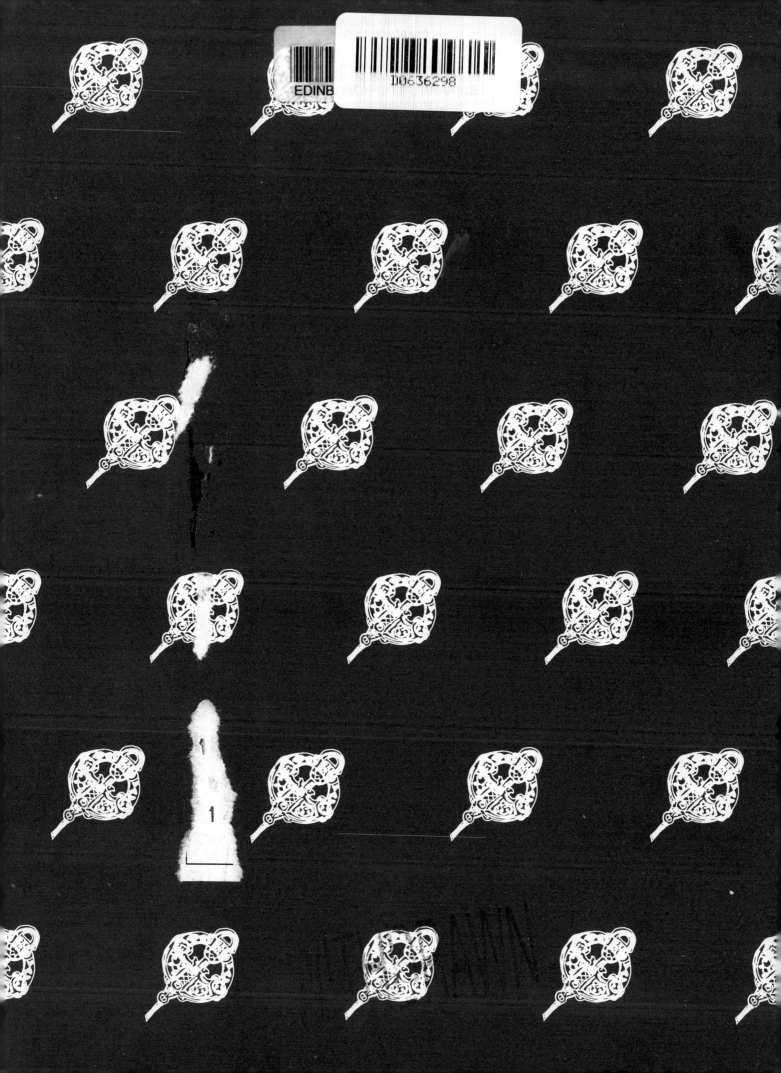

HOW *WOULD* YOU SURVIVE AS A
VIKING?

Written by
Jacqueline Morley

Illustrated by
Mark Bergin

Created & Designed by
David Salariya

W
FRANKLIN WATTS
NEW YORK•LONDON•SYDNEY

David Salariya   *Director*
Diana Holubowicz   *Editor*
Dr. Richard Hall   *Consultant*

DAVID SALARIYA

was born in Dundee, Scotland, where he studied illustration and printmaking. He has illustrated a wide range of books on botanical, historical and mythical subjects. He has created and designed many new series of books for publishers in the UK and overseas. In 1989 he established The Salariya Book Company. He lives in Brighton with his wife, the illustrator Shirley Willis.

JACQUELINE MORLEY

is a graduate of Somerville College, Oxford. She has taught English and History, and now works as a freelance translator and writer. She has written historical fiction and non-fiction for children, and has a particular interest in the history of everyday life. She has also written **Entertainment** and **Clothes** in the *Timelines* series, **An Egyptian Pyramid** in the *Inside Story* series, and **How *would* you survive as an ancient Egyptian?**

MARK BERGIN

studied illustration at Eastbourne College of Art. Since leaving art school in 1983, he has specialised in historical reconstructions and architectural cross-sections. He has illustrated four titles in the award winning *Inside Story* series and is a major contributor to the *Timelines* and *X-Ray Picture Book* series. Mark Bergin lives in East Sussex with his wife and daughter.

RICHARD A HALL BA PhD FSA MIFA

is Deputy Director of York Archaeological Trust. He has directed several large-scale excavations in York, including the internationally-known Viking site at Coppergate. He is the author of *Viking Age Archaeology in Britain and Ireland* (1991) and *The Viking Dig* (1984), as well as archaeology reports and articles. He is a Fellow of the Society of Antiquaries of London, and a past chairman of the Institute of Field Archaeologists.

©THE SALARIYA BOOK CO LTD MCMXCIII

Printed in Belgium
A CIP catalogue record for this book is available from the British Library.

First published in 1993 by Franklin Watts
This edition 1998

Franklin Watts
96 Leonard Street
London EC2A 4RH
ISBN 0 7496 1088 3
Dewey Decimal Classification Number 948

CONTENTS

BECOMING A VIKING. . .

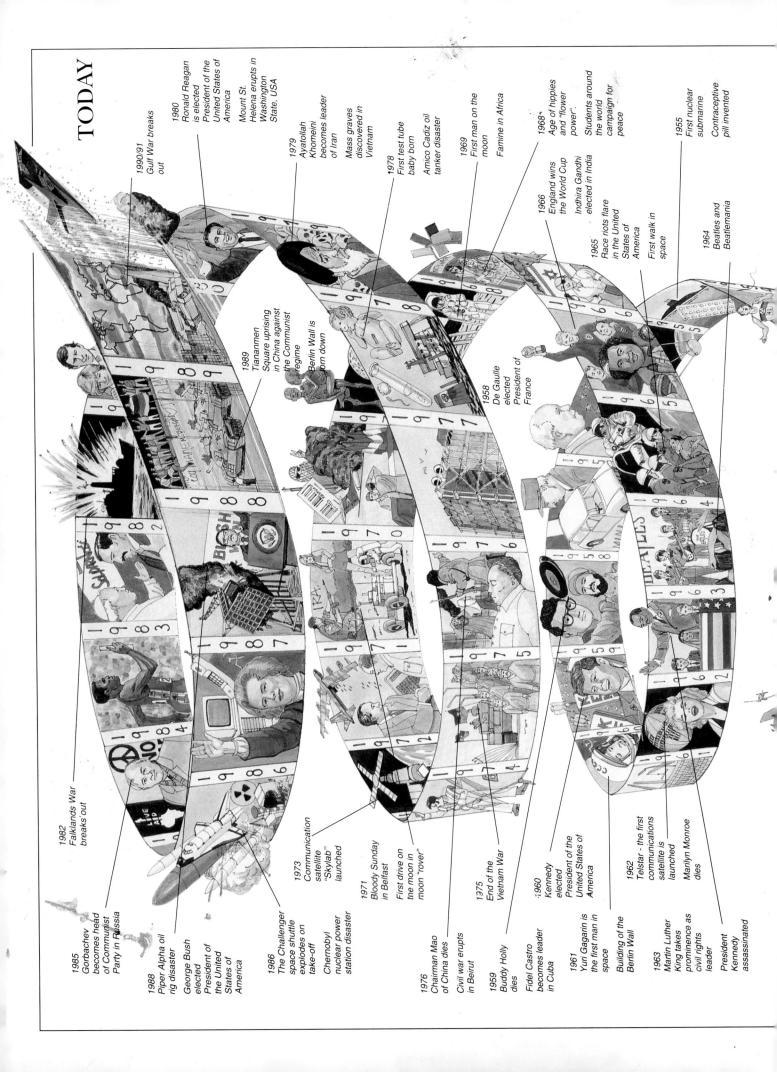

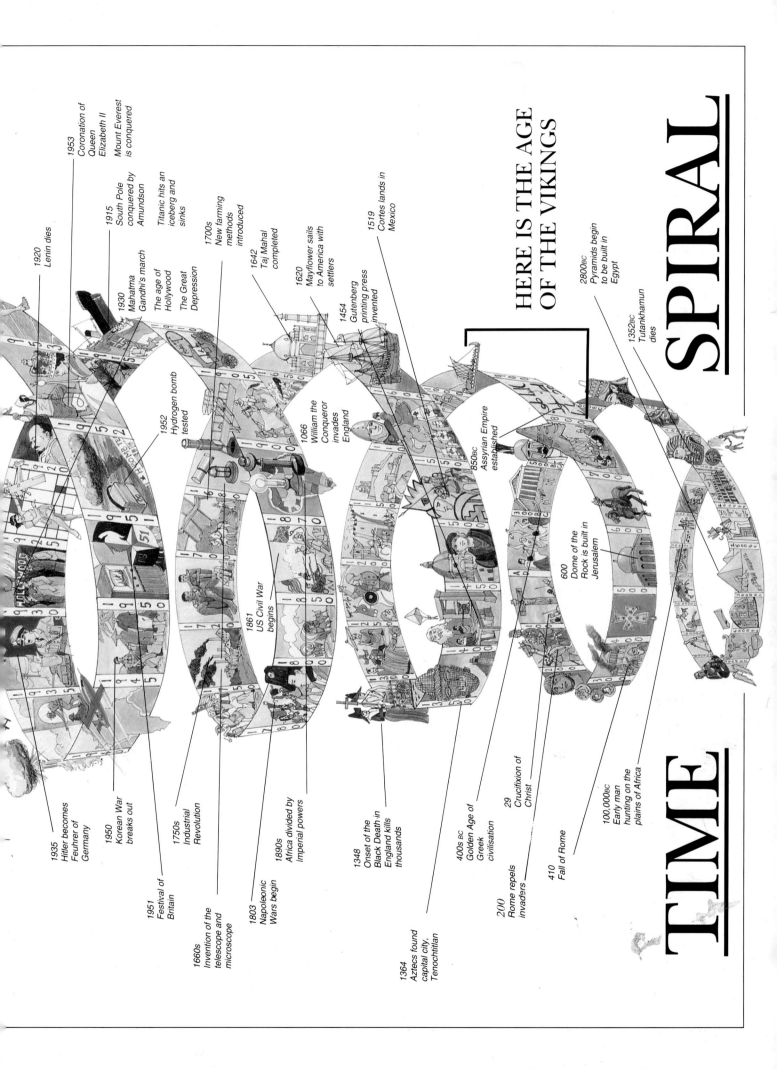

SPIRAL
TIME

HERE IS THE AGE OF THE VIKINGS

1953
Coronation of Queen Elizabeth II

Mount Everest is conquered

1920
Lenin dies

1915
South Pole conquered by Amundson

Titanic hits an iceberg and sinks

1700s
New farming methods introduced

1642
Taj Mahal completed

1620
Mayflower sails to America with settlers

1519
Cortes lands in Mexico

1930
Mahatma Gandhi's march

The age of Hollywood

The Great Depression

1454
Gutenberg printing press invented

1952
Hydrogen bomb tested

1066
William the Conqueror invades England

850BC
Assyrian Empire established

2800BC
Pyramids begin to be built in Egypt

1352BC
Tutankhamun dies

600
Dome of the Rock is built in Jerusalem

1935
Hitler becomes Feuhrer of Germany

1950
Korean War breaks out

1951
Festival of Britain

1750s
Industrial Revolution

1660s
Invention of the telescope and microscope

1803
Napoleonic Wars begin

1890s
Africa divided by imperial powers

1861
US Civil War begins

1348
Onset of the Black Death in England kills thousands

400s BC
Golden Age of Greek civilisation

29
Crucifixion of Christ

200
Rome repels invaders

410
Fall of Rome

100,000BC
Early man hunting on the plains of Africa

1364
Aztecs found capital city, Tenochtitlan

The Landscape

VAST MOUNTAINS divide the Scandinavian peninsula. Sweden, on its south-east, has fertile lowlands and vast forests which are rich in iron ore. In Norway, there are mountains which drop to the sea in many places leaving only the narrow fjords and the river valleys for farming. Denmark's flat lands, in part bare heath, are split into many islands. Iceland is a bleak place to cultivate. It is for the most part treeless, stark and barren.

The Homeland

AS A VIKING you will not be able to go shopping for everything you need – there are no shops as we know them today. For food you will have to rely on what does well locally, and most of the things you use will have to be made from what is to hand. So your homeland is of vital importance to you. In cold, harsh Greenland you will have to manage very differently from the Danish Vikings who are much further south.

The Seasons

YOU MAY FIND yourself living very far north indeed. Because of the tilt of the globe, the regions near the poles have extreme variations in the length of night and day. At midsummer in Greenland and northern Scandinavia the sun never sets and in midwinter there is no daylight. In summertime you would have a very long working day, while in winter you would spend many weeks indoors, in almost total darkness.

Hunting & Fishing

IN THE MORE northerly Viking lands you will have to rely heavily on hunting and trapping to increase your food supply. You will find the sea teeming with many different kinds of fish; there are also whales and seals to be speared, and sea birds to be shot or snared and their eggs to be gathered. The rivers are full of salmon. In Scandinavia you would be able to hunt wild boar, red deer and, in the far north, reindeer.

Viking Beliefs

UNTIL QUITE late in the Viking period (which lasted from the 9th century when Vikings began raiding, to the 11th, when they settled down) most Vikings were pagans. They worshipped gods belonging to the pagan past of the Germanic peoples. Some did convert to Christianity, yet they could still worship their pagan gods. Viking values may seem strange to you – they led hard lives and had no pity for weak people.

Viking Lifestyle

THE WORD "Viking" means piracy, or raiding. The Scandinavians had a terrifying reputation for this amongst their Christian and Slav neighbours. However you will find that many Vikings have peaceable stay-at-home lives. Being born is one of the most dangerous stages of a Viking life. If you survive that, you can expect on average to live to about fifty. Most Vikings are free, but you might be born as a slave.

BASIC FACTS ABOUT VIKING LIFE

The Wild Life

SUMMERTIME is short, and the winters are long and cold, though they may have been slightly milder in Viking times. The wild creatures around you, which are well adapted to these conditions, can be useful to you in a number of ways. The bear, the fox and the marten will provide you with warm coats and coverings, the deer and the elk will provide you with meat. Furs and hides will also provide valuable goods to sell.

The Plants & Trees

YOU MAY BE LIVING near large areas of forest, especially in Norway and Sweden. If there is not enough farmland to support everyone you may well have to cut down trees in order to create enough land to grow food. Trees are valuable. They give fuel for heating, cooking and metal-working, and timber to build houses and boats. If you cannot spare land for vegetables you will have to go out and gather wild leeks and herbs.

Viking Farming

IN DENMARK and southern Sweden your farm might be in a village. You would be able to grow wheat and barley, provided that the land is level and open. You would keep domestic animals such as pigs and cattle, but would not have to rely on them as the northern Vikings must. Only grass grows really well in the far north. There you would lead an isolated life, for wide areas of pasture are needed to support the animals of just one family.

The Language

THE VIKINGS spoke what scholars today call Old Norse, the language from which modern Norwegian, Swedish and Danish have developed. It varied little throughout Scandinavia. If you leave your Viking homeland, you will be able to talk to 'foreign' Vikings quite easily. Modern English speakers would recognise some words straight away. Egg, skill, sky and anger are just a few words the English learned from their Viking invaders.

Viking Names

MANY VIKING names are still in use now – Thora, Ingrid, Astrid, Olaf, Eric and Harald, for instance. Animal names, Ulf (wolf), Bjorn (bear) were popular, and those like Thorvald or Thorkel which referred to the thundergod Thor. The Vikings were very fond of nicknames: Harald Bluetooth, Ivar the Boneless, Radnor Lothbrok (hairy trousers), Thord the Short (he was very tall). What will they call you?

Viking Writing

THE SIGNS ABOVE spell the name Leif in Viking letters, which are called runes. The Vikings did not use pens. They cut the letters into wood. Runes were formed of straight strokes, as wood grain made curves hard to cut. Inscriptions in memory of people were cut on large stones. Here is the Viking alphabet. Choose your Viking name and see whether you can write it.

ᛁᛒᚲᚾᚦ ᚠ ᚡ ᚼ ᛁ ᚴ ᛚ ᛘ
A B C D E F G H I K L M

ᚺ ᛄ ᚴ ᚠ ᚱ ᛋᛏ ᛚ ᚼᛏᛏ
N O P Q R S T U V W X Y Z

YOUR MAP OF THE VIKING WORLD

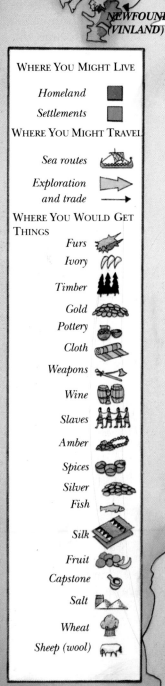

NOW THAT YOU ARE a Viking, what part of the world will you be living in? That depends on when in the Viking story you arrive. Originally the Vikings lived in the areas we now call Norway, Sweden and Denmark. Many of their descendants still live in these countries today. But from the 8th to the 11th century Viking raiders, traders and settlers made their way all over Europe and beyond. You might find yourself far from home for many months on a trading trip in Russia. In the 9th century you might be sailing with the Vikings who made new homes in the Shetland Isles, the Orkneys, the Faroes, or Iceland, or fighting beside those who seized land in England, Ireland or France. If you joined the tough fearless settlers who went to Greenland after 986, you might find yourself in America, nearly five centuries before Columbus got there.

NEWFOUNDLAND (VINLAND)

THE VIKING VIEW OF THE WORLD

The Vikings will tell you that the earth is flat, and surrounded by an ocean in which the world-serpent lies coiled. Beneath the earth is Hel, a dark and freezing place where the wicked go after their death.

THE RAINBOW makes a bridge to Asgard, the home of the gods. Viking poems describe how the ash tree, Yggdrasil, touches heavens with its branches.

One of its three roots grows beneath the earth, one reaches to Hel, and one to the mountains of the giants, which lie beyond the world's end.

WHERE YOU MIGHT LIVE

Homeland

Settlements

WHERE YOU MIGHT TRAVEL

Sea routes

Exploration and trade

WHERE YOU WOULD GET THINGS

Furs

Ivory

Timber

Gold

Pottery

Cloth

Weapons

Wine

Slaves

Amber

Spices

Silver

Fish

Silk

Fruit

Capstone

Salt

Wheat

Sheep (wool)

BEGIN YOUR NEW LIFE HERE

HERE AND ON the following pages is a panorama of the Viking world which awaits you. It is not meant to be a true-to-life picture, for you would not find all of these activities taking place at the same time. The panorama is your guide to this book. Start wherever you wish and follow the **Q** options.

WHY IS THIS shepherd taking his flock to the mountains? *Go to pages 22-23*

WHAT CROPS did the Vikings grow? To discover more about Viking farming *Go to pages 22-23*

WHAT animals did the Vikings keep? *Go to page 18* How did they feed and look after them through the winter? *Go to pages 22-23*

HOW DID the Vikings keep themselves clean? *Go to pages 38-39*

HOW DID the Vikings make bread? What else did they eat? *Go to pages 18-19*

WHAT materials did the Vikings use to build their houses? How many rooms did they have and how did they use them? *Go to pages 16-17*

HOW DID the Vikings make cloth? *Go to page 26* What is this woman using to iron the clothes? *Go to pages 20-21*

WHAT WERE rune stones and what is this man doing?
Go to page 42
Did the Vikings have an alphabet?
Go to page 7

WHAT DID A blacksmith make and how did he work?
Go to page 26

WHAT DID Viking craftsmen make and where would you expect to find their workshops?
Go to pages 24-25 and 26-27

THESE ARE iron furnaces. To find out what iron was used for
Go to pages 26-27

WHAT WAS kept in storehouses? For just a few ideas
Go to pages 16-17

WHO RULED the Viking world? What was the order of society?
Go to pages 14-15

WHAT WAS life like for Viking children? Did they go to school?
Go to pages 14-15

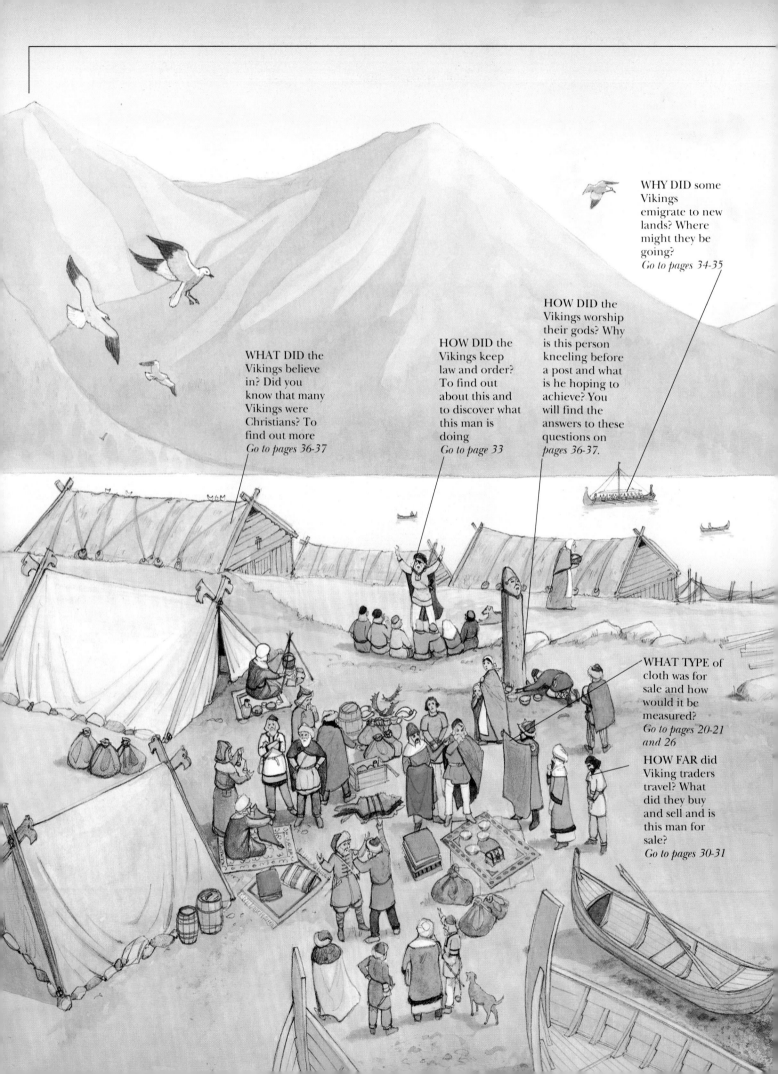

WHY DID some Vikings emigrate to new lands? Where might they be going? *Go to pages 34-35*

HOW DID the Vikings worship their gods? Why is this person kneeling before a post and what is he hoping to achieve? You will find the answers to these questions on *pages 36-37*.

WHAT DID the Vikings believe in? Did you know that many Vikings were Christians? To find out more *Go to pages 36-37*

HOW DID the Vikings keep law and order? To find out about this and to discover what this man is doing *Go to page 33*

WHAT TYPE of cloth was for sale and how would it be measured? *Go to pages 20-21 and 26*

HOW FAR did Viking traders travel? What did they buy and sell and is this man for sale? *Go to pages 30-31*

WHAT TYPES of boats did the Vikings build? What were they made from and how? *Go to pages 28-29*

WHY WERE ships so important to the Vikings? *Go to pages 28-29* Where did the Vikings sail to in their ships? *Go to pages 30-31 and 34-35*

WHAT happened to the body of a dead Viking? To find out more about Viking burials *Go to pages 40-41*

TO FIND OUT what happened when neighbours quarrelled *Go to page 32*

WHAT JOBS were carried out in winter? To find out about looking after boats and other winter jobs *Go to page 23*

WHY WAS the longship such an outstanding vessel? *Go to page 28*

HOW DID Vikings organise their raiding parties and why did they take place? *Go to page 31*

YOUR FAMILY

WHERE DO YOU FIT IN?

FAMILY HONOUR is very important. If a member is insulted by someone, the entire family is offended. If one of them does something shameful the whole family is disgraced.

This wealthy man is setting off to see how his field-workers are getting on with the harvest.

THIS IS WHAT YOUR FAMILY was like. You could count on its help in all life's difficulties. Vikings had a great sense of family loyalty. All the members looked after each other, so there were lots of aunts, uncles and cousins about.

Your father might have been a freeman. He would have owned a farm and be a follower of a powerful earl. You mother was an independent-minded woman, used to getting her own way. She had complete authority in household matters and would make all the decisions when your father was away. As the family was fairly prosperous there were several free servants to help on the farm and in the house, and some slaves as well.

You and your brothers and sisters had to work hard. You did not go to school. There were no schools. Your parents taught you all the skills you needed in life.

A Scandinavian Viking family

He spends an hour teaching his son battle skills. He shows him how to ward off blows with his shield.

He speaks at the local Thing, an assembly which decides important local issues.

The women of the family wave goodbye as he and his companions set off on a raiding trip.

Q

If someone insulted your family, what could you do about it?
Go to page 32

CHILDREN ARE EXPECTED to show plenty of spirit. If you are strong-willed and quarrelsome your parents will be pleased.

BY THE TIME you are twelve you will be ready to fend for yourself. At this age Olaf, who was later King of Norway, joined a raiding expedition.

WOMEN MAY own property, but they may not sell it without their husband's consent. They may not vote at the Thing or conduct a lawsuit.

A WOMAN IN CHARGE

She directs the farm work while her husband is away from home.

She opens the storehouse where barrels of ale, and meat are kept.

She orders a slave to take butter, cheese and three cows to market.

Some suspicious characters are seen. She leads an attack on them.

She directs the women workers as they prepare the evening meal.

Afterwards everyone gathers round as she tells a story by the fire.

YOUR PLACE IN SOCIETY
FREEMAN OR SLAVE?

THE KING WAS THE most important person in the region. He was the leader of the great landowners, or earls, who obeyed him. These earls were themselves supported by the freemen of the neighbourhood. The freemen were both farmers and warriors, for all free Vikings knew how to handle weapons. They fought for their chief in his feuds and went with him to war. He helped them in their disputes and rewarded them generously.

When they made raids together he shared out the spoils. If you were forceful and had some land you could recruit a band of followers, vow to protect them, and so become a chief yourself.

An earl

A freeman

A slave

IF YOU ARE A SLAVE, you face a life of hard work. You cannot own land, carry weapons or vote at the Thing. Your owner might give you your freedom, or allow you to buy it with extra work. Then you could become a free servant or a craftsman.

IT'S A SLAVE'S LIFE

Dawn. The first job is to check that the fire has not gone out.

Next the animals must be fed, and the stables and cow byres cleaned.

At mealtimes the slaves eat at the far end of the table.

A slave sleeps wherever he can – on the floor, or with the animals.

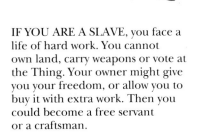

THE LIFE OF A KING

A king must have royal blood and the support of the chiefs he rules over.

He rewards his loyal followers with gifts of gold and silver and land.

Missionaries want to build a church. The king consults the Thing about this.

The king visits the most powerful earls to discuss plans for defence.

An earl in charge of a frontier region brings news of enemy invasion.

Death in battle. "Kings are made for honour not for long life."

Q

What might you get as a reward for serving your warlord?
Go to page 21

What would life be like as a farmer?
Go to page 22

YOUR HOME
WHERE WOULD YOU LIVE?

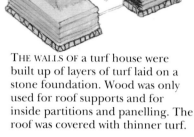

THIS IS A farmhouse in Iceland. Workrooms and storerooms open off the main living area. There would be byres, stables, barns and a smithy nearby.

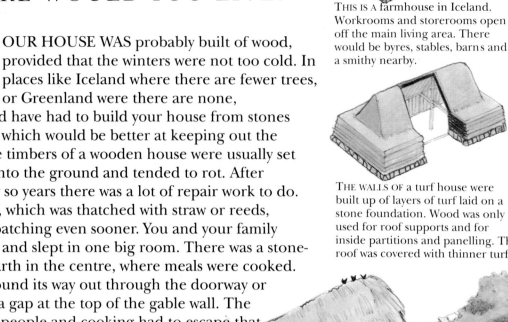

Y OUR HOUSE WAS probably built of wood, provided that the winters were not too cold. In places like Iceland where there are fewer trees, or Greenland were there are none, you would have had to build your house from stones and turf, which would be better at keeping out the cold. The timbers of a wooden house were usually set directly into the ground and tended to rot. After twenty or so years there was a lot of repair work to do. The roof, which was thatched with straw or reeds, needed patching even sooner. You and your family lived, ate and slept in one big room. There was a stone-lined hearth in the centre, where meals were cooked. Smoke found its way out through the doorway or through a gap at the top of the gable wall. The smells of people and cooking had to escape that way as well, for there were no windows to open. Low platforms along both long walls provided draught-free areas for sitting and for sleeping. You certainly had almost no privacy!

THE WALLS OF a turf house were built up of layers of turf laid on a stone foundation. Wood was only used for roof supports and for inside partitions and panelling. The roof was covered with thinner turf.

Holes are dug to take the four stout corner posts. These are braced with strong cross timbers.

The gable ends are set up. Lighter timber is used for the roof ridge and supports, and the wall-posts.

Thin rods are set between the wall-posts, leaving a gap for the door. Wattles (hazel canes) are woven through them.

The roof is thatched with straw, reeds or heather, and the floor is made of beaten earth.

Right: *Some every-day things you might use at home.*

 Q

What is booty, and where could you steal it from?
Go to page 31

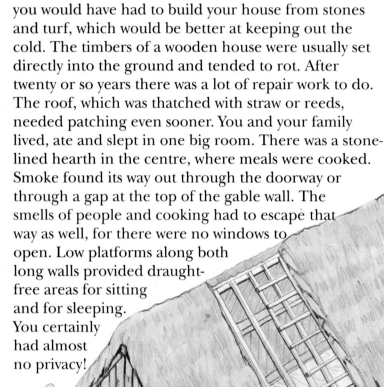

Outdoor lavatory

Smithy

A baby's chair made of slotted wooden planks.

A baby's wooden feeding bowl, with handle and spout.

A bucket made from wooden staves, with carrying handles.

Stone lamp. Whale oil or animal fat is burnt in it.

An oak storage chest strengthened with iron bands.

Why is there a cow over the doorway of this house? See page 36 for the answer.

Loom

Quern

Drying fish

Pathway of split logs

SMALLER BUILDINGS near the house are used as work-rooms, store-houses and sheds for the animals. Even if you live in a town you will keep pigs and hens, and perhaps a goat.

YOU CAN MAKE a small house quickly and economically by digging a pit and roofing it over, as the Slavs do. You will need two props and a cross-piece to hold up the roof. You may be quite snug if the soil is dry.

You did not need very much furniture. Your bed was made up directly onto the platform by the wall. Your parents might have had a proper bed, perhaps in a partitioned-off cubicle if the house was large enough.

There was a table and stools. Rich homes had cushions and wall hangings as well, and the head of the family might have had a special "high seat" with tall decorated side-posts. Your mother's loom took up quite a lot of room, but apart from these items, and some cooking jars and pans, the rest of the furniture was for storage. Food was stored in barrels of various sizes, and clothes and valuables were kept in chests.

THATCHING

Reed makes the best thatch and it is your first choice if it grows nearby. You may have to use straw or heather instead.

The reeds are harvested from the edge of lakes and rivers and sorted into bundles for the thatcher.

He sets bunches of reeds side by side in rows over battens, starting from the bottom of the roof.

Each row is held in place by thin lengths of split hazel, fastened down with bent hazel twigs.

Q

If you wanted to divorce your husband, what could you do?

Go to page 41

Why would you want to become a Christian?
Go to pages 36-37

MAKING WATTLE AND DAUB

To make wattle and daub, hazel bushes are coppiced (pruned back).

They then grow many thin stems. The thicker ones are split.

The hazel is woven in and out between strong uprights.

Mud is plastered over, to make the wall draught proof.

To make a well you dig down to reach the ground-water.

An old barrel, or planks, are used to line the well.

F O O D
WHAT WOULD YOU EAT?

THIS WAS HOW YOU would have cooked your food. But where would you have gone to buy your food? Unless you happened to live in a town where there was a market, you would have to grow your own food on your land and pick the things that you found growing wild in the forests and the land around your dwelling. You would have to keep animals such as pigs, goats and cows and kill them yourself if you wanted to eat meat. The Vikings liked to eat plenty of it! Hunting and fishing were not just sports, they were also an essential source of food. The most important elements in a Viking's diet, such as fruit, berries, meat and fish, are shown on this page.

Wheat

Fruit and nuts

Beef

Venison

Mutton

Pork

Whalemeat

Herring

Seal

Salmon

BREAD MAKING

Q

You thought you'd be dining on your own. Why have lots of people turned up to share your meal?
Go to page 32

First you have to make flour by grinding wheat or barley in a quern made from two stones.

The top stone turns on the bottom one and crushes the grain. Then mix the flour with water to make dough.

The dough is mixed in a long wooden trough. Some raw dough saved from the last baking day is added.

This has live yeasts in it which make the bread rise. The dough has to be kneaded to help it rise.

The risen dough is shaped into loaves and left to rise again. Now it is ready to be cooked.

Each loaf is set over the fire on a long-handled griddle. It will cook slowly over the hot ashes.

Preparing the food was a job done by the women of the family. If you were a girl you helped your mother almost from the time you started to walk. She would get you to stir the porridge and collect the eggs from under the hens, and send you out to look for wild leeks, mushrooms and strawberries. As you grew older you learnt to make bread, churn milk into butter, make sour-milk cheese, brew ale, wring a chicken's neck and pluck it, gut and smoke fish, and help with all the salting and pickling of meat that had to be done in the autumn when many of the cattle were killed.

If yours was a rich family, the women servants served the food at mealtimes, and filled up the tankards and drinking horns, perhaps with wine instead of ale. People used knives to cut their food, and ate it with their fingers or with a spoon if necessary.

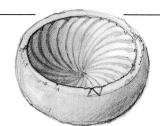

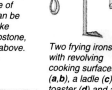

Bowls are not always made of pottery. It can be easier to make them of soapstone, like the one above.

Striking a light. A steel striker (above) is struck on a flint to make sparks (right).

Two frying irons with revolving cooking surfaces (**a,b**), a ladle (**c**), a toaster (**d**) and a fork (**e**) for skewering meat.

Wooden troughs are carved at home. Someone has enjoyed decorating these ends, shown in detail.

A bucket made of wooden staves banded with iron. Its wide base makes it less easy to knock over.

COOKING MEAT

Most meat is grilled or roasted. How would you cook a very big piece of meat?

Dig a pit in the ground and line it with wood. Meanwhile some large stones heat on the fire.

Fill the pit with water and lower the joint of meat into it. Add salt and herbs for a good flavour.

Drop hot stones into the pit, to bring the water to the boil. A 4.5 kg joint cooks in three hours like this.

You could also bake food in a hole packed with hot embers and covered with earth to keep in the heat.

The best meat is roasted on a spit. You have to turn the spit fairly often to cook the meat evenly.

Q

Where could you get a new pair of soft leather shoes? *Go to page 27*

What would you do in the evenings after supper? *Go to page 14*

CLOTHES
WHAT WOULD YOU WEAR?

First she puts on a finely pleated linen petticoat with wide loose sleeves. This reaches her feet.

Then she adds a shorter, open-sided overdress and fastens its straps with large oval brooches.

Over this she puts a long woollen shawl which she pins together at her throat with a third big brooch.

Q

How did Vikings get hold of cloth and silk from the East?
Go to page 30

YOU NEEDED really warm clothes for the Scandinavian climate, at least for most of the year. You might be a farmer out of doors in all weathers, or a merchant battling with wind and rain by land or sea. Even stay-at-home townsmen and womenfolk had to fetch water, chop wood, pen animals and do all sorts of other outdoor jobs in ice and snow. Your clothes would almost all be home made, either by you or your servants.

What could you use to make them? Your sheep provided wool from which to make warm cloth. This was a lengthy process which occupied the women of the household for much of the year. If you could get to a large market you could buy very fine woollen cloth imported from Frisia and silk from the Far East, but these were very expensive.

The tough fibres of the flax plant were spun and woven into linen for underclothes. This was hard work, for the flax had to be well beaten first, to make the fibres fit for use. For waterproof protection you needed animal skins, and for real warmth, furs.

You will want to decorate your clothes with bands of patterned ribbon. See page 26 to find out how these are made.

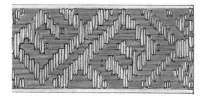

How will you iron your clothes? The whale-bone board and the heated glass ball shown (below right) could be an ironing board and iron.

BUSY HOUSEWIVES and mothers need clothes that are practical. The loosely hanging over-tunic and pleated linen petticoat can easily be drawn aside when your baby needs to be breastfed.

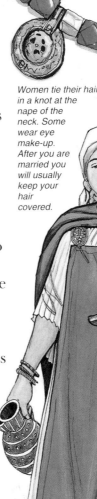

Women tie their hair in a knot at the nape of the neck. Some wear eye make-up. After you are married you will usually keep your hair covered.

This is how you would be dressed as a prosperous married woman. You have fine jewellery and your overdress is richly decorated with a woven panel.

A necklace of cornelian and crystal beads, hung with trinkets brought back from the Far East.

Luxurious gold buckle. Most brooches are of silver or copper-alloy.

An oval dress buckle. These varied a lot in quality. You will want to wear the best you can afford.

Nail cleaner and ear scoop. They were worn hanging from women's brooches, like keys.

How to copy a brooch cheaply, using very little metal. Make a baked-clay mould of the face of the brooch.

Line it with cloth dipped in clay. Press more clay against it to form the back of the mould.

Separate the pieces and remove the cloth. This leaves a thin gap into which molten metal can be poured.

There is no soap.
Ammonia from
cows' urine is used.
It is a good cleaning
agent.

Clothes are washed
in running water or
rinsed in ammonia.

You were glad of leggings and long skirts. Viking houses could be both stuffy and draughty. Women wore knee-length cloth leggings under their skirts in cold weather. Both men and women wore heavy cloaks and fur wraps for winter. No matter how cold the weather was you always pinned your cloak so that your sword arm was uncovered and you could reach your sword at a moment's notice.

A man's massive neck-ring made of almost 2 kg of gold. It might be your reward for serving your warlord.

Long leggings are worn under the tunic. They can be tight, or loose like trousers, in which case you might bind them to your legs with bands of cloth or leather.

Three-lobed brooches, often worn at the neck, are popular.

Shoes are made of leather. Some winter shoes have the hair left on them for extra warmth. This winter ankle boot might be worn for skating.

THIS RICH VIKING merchant has travelled abroad. His clothes are influenced by the styles of the Slav peoples of central Europe. He has a fur-trimmed hat and enormously wide trousers bound tightly to his legs below the knees. His cloak is fastened with a big ring-and-pin brooch.

VIKING CHILDREN wear clothes in very much the same style as their parents'. Girls wear pinafore dresses like their mothers', and boys wear leather or woollen jerkins and leggings. Indoors they wear soft leather shoes or sandals. Outside they wrap up in warm woollen cloaks and boots. Rich children have fur-lined cloaks and fur hats and mits.

Slaves and poor people wear plain rough woollen tunics. They tie cloth or skins around their feet for shoes.

Q

How would you make wool into cloth?
Go to page 26

How would you keep yourself clean?
Go to pages 38-39

FARMING IN ICELAND

HOW WOULD YOU LIVE AND WORK?

The year begins in April when the snows melt. It is time for ploughing and for sowing the barley and oats.

A S A VIKING FARMER you had to make your land provide the best living for your family. If you lived in Scandinavia there was enough sunshine to grow oats and barley, and perhaps some rye and wheat. You could keep enough livestock for your own needs and use the rest of your land to grow cereals to sell.

But suppose you lived in Iceland, where oats and barley grow with difficulty, or Greenland where they will not grow at all? Then you had to live off the grasslands.

This meant relying on hunting and fishing and on rearing cattle and sheep. These animals needed plenty of pasture so you needed more land than the southern Vikings did.

IN THE SUMMER, some of the family stay at the sheiling, a small house in the mountains. They take the herds there to find better grass.

In early spring the walls around the home-meadow are repaired, where frost has damaged them.

Towards the end of May the lambs are old enough to be taken from their mothers. The adult sheep are shorn of their fleece.

At the coast May and June are the time for gathering eggs from millions of sea birds that nest on the cliffs.

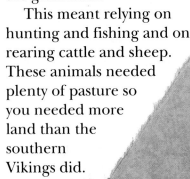

Q

Where can you get a new set of knives made?
Go to page 26

If you were a farmer and there was no land to spare, what could you do?
Go to pages 34-35

At the sheiling in midsummer the animals yield lots of milk. Butter and curd cheeses are made.

The dairy produce is sent to the coast on pack-horses, where it will be sold, or traded for salt or fish.

August is haymaking month. Not only the hay meadow but every small patch of long grass is cut.

In late August and early September the corn is cut. The cattle are allowed to eat the remaining stubble.

In October the herds are rounded up in readiness for winter. Some may have strayed many miles.

Fuel has to be laid in for the long dark winter months. Trees are felled and slabs of peat are cut.

The first settlers in Iceland claimed so much land that there was often little left for late-comers. Even so, your farm was isolated. The best site was at the foot of the mountains, and close to the lowland. There you had shelter from the harsh winters and easy access to the mountain grass in summer.

Claiming your land. A man is allowed as much land as he can walk round in a day, carrying a torch. A woman has to drive a cow along with her.

YOU ARE A FARMER'S WIFE

In the morning you drive the boar to the home meadow to fatten. He alone is allowed to eat the best grass.

You have to supervise the housework, the pigs and poultry. Today there is fish to cook, gut and dry as well.

Weaving takes all your spare time. Cloth is one of the few things Icelanders can offer foreign traders.

Grass grows on the turf roof

Your farmhouse was built of turf, on a stone base, and the rooms were lined with wood. The long main room had several others opening from it. These could serve as bedrooms or weaving rooms, or they might house the dairy or lavatory. You also needed warm houses for the animals in winter, barns to store hay, and a smithy. These were grouped around the farmhouse. In front of the farm was the home meadow, which was walled to prevent the animals from eating its carefully tended grass. It was the main source of hay which kept the cattle alive in winter.

In the evening you do the milking. At busy times, like hay-making, you have to work hard in the fields.

Q

You've got a juicy joint of meat from the autumn slaughter. How will you cook it?
Go to page 19

What rights do women have?
Go to page 14

Some animals have to be killed each autumn. There is not enough hay for them all. The meat is packed in salt.

This is the time for having feasts and celebrating weddings, for there is plenty of fresh meat to eat.

Animals cannot pass winter nights outdoors, but in the day sheep and goats nibble grass through the snow.

Cows are more delicate. They are kept in houses, called byres, day and night in winter and fed there.

The long dark winter is the time for indoor work, like making and mending tools, and repairing boats.

Animal skins from the autumn slaughter are made into warm clothing, shoes and bed-covers.

LIFE IN A TOWN
WHAT WOULD YOU FIND THERE?

THERE WERE many advantages to town life. You would not have had complete control over your food supply, since much that you needed came from the country, but this was only a draw back in times of famine. You found plenty of country people in the market, wanting to sell you food. Towns were, above all, places where people met to do trade. This was how towns came into being in the first place. At Hedeby, for instance (today in Northern Germany) you met merchants of all kinds – some with amber and furs from the Northern Baltic, others from Norway and Sweden with soapstone bowls, reindeer hides, and cargoes of bog-iron. There were also Frankish traders with fine goldsmith's work, cloth merchants from Frisia (modern Holland), and some adventurous traders who came north through Russia, bringing silks and spices and looking for slaves.

If you were a craftsman hoping to earn a good living, the town was the place to be. Craftsmen's workshops lined the streets, with goods set out to catch the eye of wealthy passers-by.

A missionary, Ansgar, came to Hedeby in 827 and was allowed to build a church. He did not make many converts.

TOWNS often have a mint, authorised by the king to issue coins. Above are two silver coins made at Hedeby.

In the tenth century King Harald Bluetooth built a rampart round the town to protect it from attack.

In 1050 the town was burned by Norwegian Vikings. Sixteen years later it was destroyed by a Slav people, the Wends.

Q

Why would anyone want to colonise a remote place like Staraja Ladoga?
Go to page 30

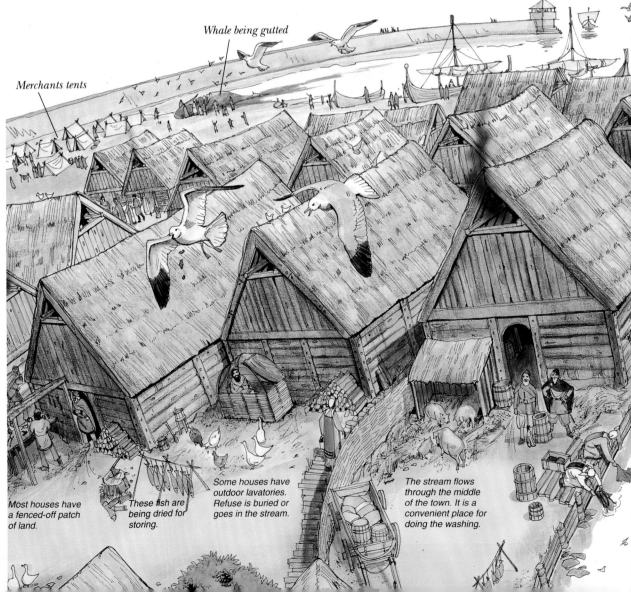

Whale being gutted

Merchants tents

Most houses have a fenced-off patch of land.

These fish are being dried for storing.

Some houses have outdoor lavatories. Refuse is buried or goes in the stream.

The stream flows through the middle of the town. It is a convenient place for doing the washing.

THIS IS the town of Staraja Ladoga. Although it is far away in northern Russia, the land of the Finns and Slavs, some of it has been built by Vikings. They come mostly from Sweden and find it convenient to have a base here.

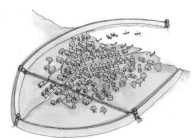

Farmers meet to buy and sell livestock. They bring surplus butter, cheese and grain to sell in the market.

Towns were encouraged and protected by ambitious kings. In return for protecting its inhabitants and for allowing the market to be held, a king received a proportion of the profits made there – a tax, in fact. Kings needed plenty of money to pay their followers and keep their power. As one of the townspeople you would have benefited from the arrangement. A town without the backing of an army was at the mercy of sea pirates (possibly Vikings from other regions!) or foreign invaders, whilst a well-defended one attracted merchants from far and near and became more and more prosperous.

THIS IS a view of Hedeby looking towards the harbour. The wall extends into the water to make a safe haven. Some visiting merchants have pitched tents by the shore.

Godfred sited his new town where the route used by merchants from the south met those of sea traders from east and west.

You can buy shoes, saddlery, weapons, jewellery and tools from the craftsmen's market stalls.

Merchant ships

Merchants bring goods from afar: swords, glass, wine and silk from the south; ivory, furs and slaves from the north.

In the slave market you will be sold Christians. They are hard to sell abroad. Other Christians will not deal in them.

Q

You want to have a steam bath. How can you do this?
Go to page 38

There are plenty of country sights and smells in the town. People keep pigs and poultry and even cows in their back yards.

Hedeby is a large town by Viking standards. This view shows only a section. Many houses have storage sheds and workshops alongside.

The smith works iron by heating and hammering it. His assistant raises the heat of the fire with bellows.

He makes all the iron products that you need: knives, axes, cooking pans, keys, and padlocks like the one shown above.

If you want a high quality sword that will not bend you must go to a smith who knows the art of damascening.

He will heat iron rods until their surface turns to steel, and then twist several rods together to mingle the steel and iron.

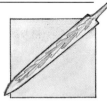

When the metal is hammered, the iron and paler steel form a pattern. Such a blade deserves a finely decorated hilt.

C R A F T S
MAKING THE THINGS YOU NEED

MANY OF THE THINGS that you used were homemade. You were expected to know how to use your hands. The men of the household knew how to fell trees, cut up the timber and shape it into gates and fences, tools, carts, sledges and furniture.

Many farmers had their own smithies, where they made and mended iron tools and vessels. You needed these skills if you lived in a remote area. Where farms were reasonably close together you might be visited by a travelling blacksmith.

Part of a piece of tapestry. Wealthy Vikings hang tapestry on their walls for warmth.

The warp threads, kept taut by hanging weights, are separated into two layers, one attached to the heddle-bar. By moving the bar you lift alternate layers and pass the weft thread between them.

Skilled smiths specialise in decorative work. This axe is being prepared to take an inlay of contrasting metal.

The pattern is marked on the iron blade in grooves. Silver wire is then hammered into the grooves.

All women are trained in a craft, for they are the cloth makers. Even in the wealthiest families girls are taught to spin and weave. For most women carding, spinning, weaving, dyeing, cutting and stitching make a never-ending job. They not only clothe the family but produce bedclothes, wall-hangings and sails for the ships.

a
b
c

Cloth-making tools:
a. iron-toothed comb for disentangling the fibres of the sheep's clipped fleece;
b. cutting shears;
c. reel onto which newly-spun thread is wound.

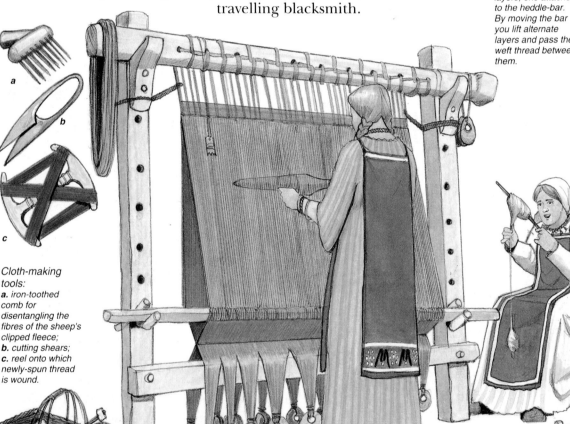

Loom weights

WOMEN'S CRAFTS

Viking women are skilled embroiderers. Patterned braid is woven by passing warp threads of various colours through holes in a series of wooden or antler tablets.

To work, the weaver ties one end of the work around her waist, and the other end to something fixed. She twists the tablets to vary the warp positions and produce the design.

This woman is pushing the weft into place. Her companion spins from a distaff.

Cloth is sold in body measurements. An ell, for instance, is the length from your elbow to your fingertips. Don't buy from someone with short arms!

MAKING JEWELLERY

Brooches are made by pouring molten bronze or pewter into moulds. This is a mould of carved soapstone.

A pendant decorated with filagree. If you buy it, ask if it is pure gold or silver or only coated.

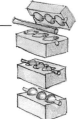

Filagree patterns are made of wire which has been melted in a heated mould to form a string of tiny beads.

MAKING AN ANTLER COMB

Use the antler of the red deer. This makes a strong comb. Cut a piece to the length of the comb you want.

From this cut two long plates to form the comb's back. These can be ornamented with a pattern of cut lines.

Bone carvers sell many small decorative objects. This figure is a playing piece for a board game.

Useful things made from bone: *a*. a name tagmarked in runes; *b*. a comb (with some teeth missing); *c*. a pin.

Now cut a series of small plates from spare pieces of antler. These will form the teeth of the comb.

Drill holes in the plates and the back pieces. Assemble the comb and secure it with small iron pins.

A bone carver. He sells his goods directly from his work stall.

If you wanted something out of the ordinary, perhaps to give as a present – a silver brooch, a bead necklace or a decorated sword – you had to go to a town. There you could see these things being made by craftsmen who sold them from their workshops. You could watch them carving bone, amber and jet, and making multi-coloured beads by fusing fragments of different coloured glass. If you preferred a quiet steady life to a risky one, you might decide to make a living as a craftsman.

Now that the small plates are securely held, you will find it easy to saw each into several teeth.

OTHER CRAFTSMEN

Leather-workers supply things that need to be tough yet pliable, like shoes, belts and harnesses. Fine items often have raised designs on them. This is called embossing.

Soapstone, a soft rock which is found in natural outcrops, has many uses. The required shape is cut in the rock-face and detached by undercutting.

The craftsman may take the soapstone piece home to finish. He makes lamps, cooking pots, bowls, loom-weights, and moulds for metal casting.

CRAFTS **27**

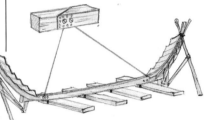

CONSTRUCTING A LONGSHIP

A SKILFUL SHIPBUILDER watches growing trees and notes which will give the shapes he needs. Oak logs are split into wedge-shaped pieces to provide planks. Pine is split vertically and gives fewer logs.

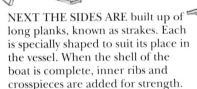

THE KEEL, which is the ship's backbone, is laid down first. Curved stems at each end form the prow at the front of the ship and sternpost at the rear. They are attached to the keel by overlapping joints.

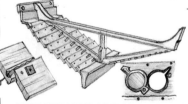

NEXT THE SIDES ARE built up of long planks, known as strakes. Each is specially shaped to suit its place in the vessel. When the shell of the boat is complete, inner ribs and crosspieces are added for strength.

THE STRAKES ARE JOINED with iron nails, backed with a roving. Caulking, made of tarred wool, is packed between the strakes to make them watertight. Oarholes are cut and given pivoting covers.

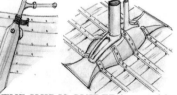

THE SHIP IS GUIDED by a rudder like a large paddle which is attached to the stern on the starboard or right side. The bottom of the mast is held steady by a huge block of wood known, from its shape, as the mastfish.

IF YOU WERE ASKED what you most longed to own, as a Viking you would almost certainly reply "a really fine ship". Vikings were justifiably proud of their skills in shipbuilding and seamanship. They were famous throughout the northern seas for making boats that were exceptionally swift and strong, yet supple enough to withstand the battering of ocean waves, and also shallow enough to travel far inland along rivers. Sailing was part of daily life. Not knowing how to sail was even more of a disadvantage to a Viking than not knowing how to drive a car today.

Your father would have taught you to row and to handle the sail of a small boat when you were very young.

If you wanted anything better than a rough workboat, you went to a professional shipbuilder. He showed you his timber, sometimes stored under water to prevent warping, and told you that the best ships were made of oak. He might use pine or birch instead, but the keel, or backbone of the ship, which gives the ship its strength, was always made of oak.

Knorr

The knorr is a sturdy cargo-boat built to withstand rough seas. The river boat is a small workboat that can hoist a sail.

River boat

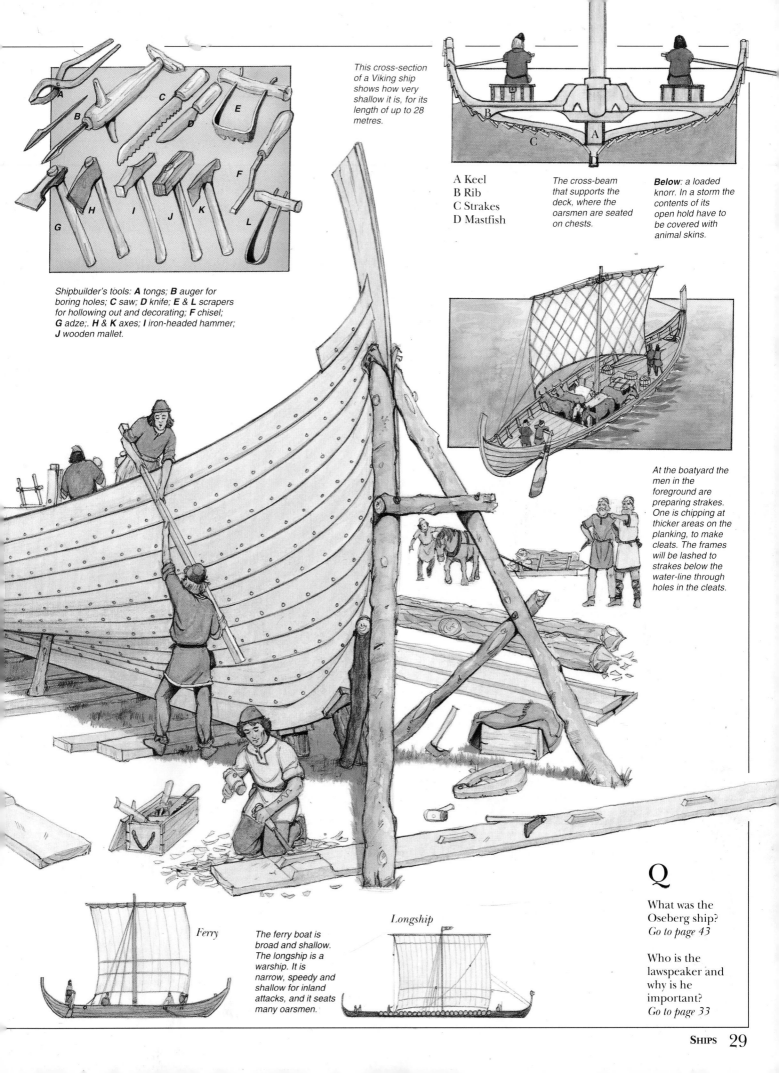

Shipbuilder's tools: **A** tongs; **B** auger for
boring holes; **C** saw; **D** knife; **E** & **L** scrapers
for hollowing out and decorating; **F** chisel;
G adze;. **H** & **K** axes; **I** iron-headed hammer;
J wooden mallet.

This cross-section of a Viking ship shows how very shallow it is, for its length of up to 28 metres.

A Keel
B Rib
C Strakes
D Mastfish

The cross-beam that supports the deck, where the oarsmen are seated on chests.

Below: a loaded knorr. In a storm the contents of its open hold have to be covered with animal skins.

At the boatyard the men in the foreground are preparing strakes. One is chipping at thicker areas on the planking, to make cleats. The frames will be lashed to strakes below the water-line through holes in the cleats.

Ferry

The ferry boat is broad and shallow. The longship is a warship. It is narrow, speedy and shallow for inland attacks, and it seats many oarsmen.

Longship

Q

What was the Oseberg ship?
Go to page 43

Who is the lawspeaker and why is he important?
Go to page 33

MERCHANTS
WHAT CAN YOU SELL?

IF YOU OWNED a trading boat you were able to swell your fortune by bringing back goods from foreign lands to sell at home. You could share a boat with a group of companions and make your plans together. You might decide to go to one of the big Viking trading cities – Hedeby, for instance – where one met merchants bringing luxury goods from the south – fine textiles and tableware, jewellery and glass, Frankish swords and Rhenish wine.

You could sail even further north-east along the Baltic coast to get furs, ropes made of walrus hide, walrus ivory and slaves. The slaves were captives who had been seized in the surrounding Slav lands. Your companions would help you to round up some which you could sell at a profit by taking them south along the Russian rivers.

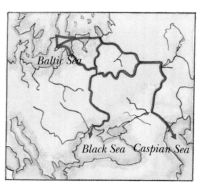

Leaving Staraja Ladoga, you sail upstream in small boats laden with slaves, honey, wax and furs to sell.

When you reach the river's source you drag the boats overland to get to another river flowing south.

You reach Kiev, where many Vikings have settled, and you trade with Arabs bringing silks and spices from the south.

You may seek your fortune even further down to the Black Sea, and on to the splendid city of Constantinople.

Viking river routes led from the Baltic to the Black Sea and the Caspian Sea.

Q

What is a byre, and what would you put in it?
Go to page 23

Why has your neighbour hung fish up outside his house?
Go to page 24

A SLAVE'S FATE

A Slav or Celtic family is captured by Viking raiders.

Men and women are led in chains to the Viking boats.

The Church may pay for captured Christians to save them.

On trading trips slaves are useful to do the hard work.

Slaves can be bartered for goods in foreign lands.

Or sold in Viking markets, like Hedeby, for home use.

R A I D E R S
WOULD YOU MAKE A FORTUNE?

The earl and his men form a raiding fellowship. They swear loyalty to one another.

Y our companions could have suggested a much more exciting way of getting rich quickly. They had heard that a powerful earl in your area had just returned from a raiding party in one of the Christian lands over the sea. The people of these lands were wealthy, it seemed, with plenty of gold, silver and fine furnishings in their houses, which could easily be taken from them in a quick surprise attack. Monasteries were good defenceless targets that provided rich pickings – holy goblets and garments and richly jewelled boxes for storing relics and books. The earl was planning to go again soon, and was looking for supporters to join him. Last time his followers returned laden with treasure, as well as Christian slaves. Encampments in the Anglo-Saxon and Frankish lands were set up so that raids could be launched from a fixed base. A strong leader could take over large areas of land, which would provide good farming for Viking settlers.

Each man brings his own fighting gear – sword, spear, shield, broad-axe and helmet.

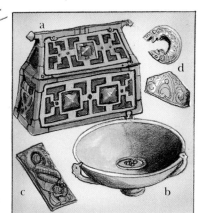

Surprise is your strong point. The shallow ships go far up rivers, enabling you to pounce on inland towns.

Landing is easy anywhere. The boat is run ashore and everyone leaps out as soon as the keel scrapes the ground.

You will have to be ruthless when foreigners beg you not to kill them.

SOME OBJECTS found in Scandinavia which were probably seized as booty on raids: **a**. a Scottish or Irish reliquary looted to make a jewel box: **b**. a silver dish that was formerly a sacred church vessel; **c**. a book-mount used as a brooch; **d**. a gold scabbard end and belt end, both of Celtic workmanship.

The ships were built so that both people and horses could get on them and off them easily.

Local horses are seized in order to load the booty, round up slaves and gallop back to the waiting ships.

The ship would tilt gracefully to one side to let the animals off yet would remain stable and afloat.

You are wounded by a desperate Anglo-Saxon farmer.

You are helped away. What will happen to you next?

Q

Your ship is caught in a storm. Whom can you turn to for help?
Go to page 36

WHO DECIDES?

Your cousin, who is sarcastic, says something scornful to an acquaintance, who draws a sword and kills him.

You rush to tell his parents. The family discuss whether or not to accept payment for the wrong. They decide on revenge.

They kill a relative of the killer. In return your father is killed because he is head of your cousin's family.

After many months of killing the families let judges settle the dispute and decide the compensation.

 Q

You are a farmer and have some livestock you want to sell. Where should you go?
Go to page 25

THE VIKING CODE OF HONOUR was very strict. You had to obey it or you were despised by everyone. The most important rule was to be fearless and loyal. Nothing was baser than treachery. You supported your family or your leader without weighing the rights and wrongs of the matter.

Quarrelling families could soon find themselves involved in a blood feud, as each sought vengeance by killing members of the other. The feud might end in a house burning. The men of one clan surprised the members of a family belonging to another in their home, surrounded the house, and set it on fire, giving the people inside the choice of burning to death or coming out and having all their menfolk slaughtered.

GROUNDS FOR divorce: blood ties are more important than those of marriage. One woman divorced her husband because he was friendly with her brother's killer.

VIKING VALUES

Honour. There is no deeper disgrace than being a coward. You must be ready to fight anyone who speaks ill of you or your family. You must support the lord to whom you have sworn loyalty. You must never surrender, but fight with your comrades until the end.

Generosity. Kings and earls reward their followers with gifts, for to give freely is the sign of a noble spirit. Even the poorest person would be ashamed to be stingy. You must welcome travellers and give them food, shelter and protection. You may need the same one day.

Vigilance. Danger is never far away. The river may flood; pirates may attack; neighbours may seek revenge; there may be foreign enemies in the land. You will not last long unless you are ready for all comers. There is a saying: the wise man is never parted from his weapons.

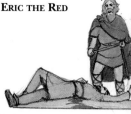

WOMEN CANNOT speak at the Thing, but whole families come to the big annual meeting and camp while it lasts.

THE LAW IS not written down. Each year the Lawspeaker recites a third of it, so that people remember it.

YOU CAN TRADE and enjoy sport at the Thing. Wrestling and horse-fighting are popular.

In 982 Eric the Red, an Icelandic settler from Norway, quarrels with a nearby farmer and kills him.

He is brought before the Thing. Thirty-six judges hear his case and banish him for three years.

Apart from their feuding the Vikings were not lawless. They accepted the authority of traditional laws. Legal decisions were made by the freemen of the district at a meeting called the Thing. Judges imposed penalties for wrong doing, based on a scale of payments. The highest was for killing a man, a lesser sum for chopping off his nose, and so on. Though judgement was made by the Thing it was up to you to make the offender pay up. If you were bringing a lawsuit, you needed to take friends along to back you up. Decisions tended to be made in favour of the more powerful side. It paid to be the follower of a strong chief; he would support you.

He goes fishing and exploring with some friends. They find a land mostly frozen over, and spend the time there.

He names it Greenland, to persuade others to join him there. In 986 the first storm-tossed settlers arrive.

Comradeship. Friends swear to be loyal to each other with a solemn oath and by clasping hand. Such an oath makes them as close as members of your family. Groups of friends clasp hands to form a fellowship for a joint purpose – a raid perhaps.

Ruthlessness. You do not spare enemies who would destroy you if they could. You do not rear sickly babies who may become sickly adults. Once when there was a famine in Iceland the old and the sick were thrown over cliffs. You can not afford to be kind.

Rough Justice. Disagreements can be settled by a fight. Whoever wins is thought to have had right on his side. Duels, fought with swords and shields, are held where three roads meet. Wooden shields splinter easily, so each contestant is allowed three.

Q

What did the Arabs think of the way the Vikings lived?
Go to page 38

*Overland travel is
easier in winter,
when horse-drawn
sledges can
glide easily over
the snow.*

*You will have to use
skis if you are
going any distance
on foot, or you
may sink into a
snowdrift.*

*Skaters strap
lengths of bone to
their shoes and
push themselves
along the frozen
rivers with spiked
sticks.*

*To make it easy to
move goods, carts
and sledges have
removable bodies
that can be loaded
onto boats.*

Q

Did the Vikings
have a code of
honour?
Go to pages 32-33

You've heard a
story about
someone who
was killed by a
shaft of
mistletoe! Can
this be true?
Go to page 37

*People travel on
horse back if they
can afford it. There
are a few good
roads and bridges
on important routes.*

*Most rivers have to
be forded at shallow
points. These are
sometimes marked
by standing stones.*

*Carts are used to
carry goods.
Women may travel
in them but men like
to ride horses.*

TRAVELLING
HOW WOULD YOU TRAVEL?

AS A VIKING YOU might have had to
make some long journeys. You needed
to know how to ride, ski and skate,
and how to handle a boat, a cart and
a sledge. Men often left home on long trips,
and came back with booty, bought or stolen.
But there were some journeys from which
people did not expect to return. Like it or
not, you might have to leave your
homeland. When your father died your
eldest brother took over the farm. If there
was no land to spare, or you could not
afford to buy any, you had to seek an emptier
country, perhaps on the very edge of the
world. The people below are setting off from
Norway for a new life in Iceland. They are
taking waterproof skins and food for the journey
which may last more than a week, tools for
metal-working and carpentry, animals for
their farms, and slaves.

SAILING WEST

*How will you know in which direction to sail
when you are at sea? You do not have a
compass to tell you which way your boat is
pointing; the Vikings did not know about the
magnetic north. Whenever possible you
keep the coast in sight and look out for well
known land-marks.*

*On the open sea you will have to watch the
position of the sun or the stars. When the
sun seems highest, it is due south. This high
point will be closer to the horizon the further
north you sail. By measuring this distance,
you will be able to judge how far north
you are.*

*There are many other signs which may help
you to judge a ship's position. Cloud
formations and the flight of sea birds can
show that land is just over the horizon.
Alterations in the waves suggest changes of
depth, and the presence of currents and
underwater rocks.*

On the long voyage to a new home you have to sleep wherever you can, huddled under skins. There is no shelter in storms.

As the boat nears land you throw overboard the posts of your high seat. They will guide you to your new home.

At your journey's end you search for a sheltered landing place. Then you unload and lead out the animals.

One of the first things you will want is a hot meal. It has not been possible to cook on board ship.

Left: finds that prove the sagas have some truth.

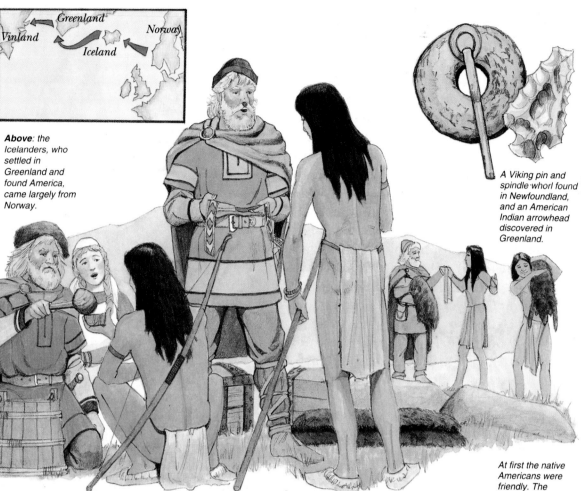

Greenland
Vinland   *Norway*
Iceland

Above: the Icelanders, who settled in Greenland and found America, came largely from Norway.

A Viking pin and spindle-whorl found in Newfoundland, and an American Indian arrowhead discovered in Greenland.

You will have to live in a tent at first. If you have not brought one you can use timber and animal skins.

Following the will of the gods, you make the new farm on the spot where the posts you threw overboard have come ashore.

At first the native Americans were friendly. The skraelings, as the Vikings called them, were pleased to part with furs of fine quality in return for pieces of red cloth.

You would have heard many tales of the heroes who sailed west. They discovered Iceland in about 860. The fishing there was so good that the first settlers did little else. Because they forgot to make hay their cattle died of starvation in the winter and they had to return to Norway. The families that went there later were wiser. They made successful farms in the grassy areas. Unfortunately there was soon not enough to go round. People were forced to look further, to harsh, treeless Greenland, and even beyond.

Aud the Deep Minded, a widowed noblewoman, led her dependents to Iceland and handed out land like a chief.

The sagas say America was sighted in 986 by a man called Bjarni, who had been blown off course on his way to Greenland. Wanting to reach his goal he did not go ashore. In about 990 Leif the Lucky, son of Eric the Red, bought Bjarni's boat and, following his directions, reached the unknown land.

He arrived somewhere in the region of Labrador and sailed south till he came to a land with rich grass and waters full of salmon. He decided to spend the winter there and sent his crew exploring. One man rushed back with amazing news. He had found grapes growing wild!

When Leif came home with news of this land many Greenlanders were eager to settle there. Several attempts were made, including one led by a man named Thorfinn. His followers spent three years there, but the natives grew hostile and forced the out-numbered Vikings to leave.

Q

Where would you look for Asgard and the world-serpent? *Go to page 8*

RELIGION
WHAT DO YOU BELIEVE?

Animals are sacrificed to the gods at festivals. People put their offerings on poles outside their houses.

Local chiefs lead the worship in their own houses or out of doors, in sacred groves of trees.

Thor the thunder god is friendly to humans. You can call on his help in an emergency, as this sailor is doing.

Frey ensures prosperity and makes humans and animals fertile. Wedding toasts are drunk in his honour.

Q

Why would anyone want to bury a ship?
Go to page 41

You are a slave and you've just been bought. What sort of life will you have?
Go to pages 15, 30 and 31

A S A VIKING, you had to decide whether or not to become a Christian. The Vikings worshipped many gods. The Christians had only one god, but to judge from the prosperity of Christian countries and the splendour of their churches, this god was very powerful. You would have heard of him from Vikings who had been abroad, or perhaps from Frankish missionaries. You might have wanted to add this Christian god to the Viking ones, but the missionaries did not like that. Merchants found that it paid to be Christian, for Christians liked to trade with other Christians.

You could compromise by letting them make the sign of the cross over you. This was not a proper baptism so you could still worship your own gods, but it made you Christian enough to do business with.

If you bow down with gifts before images of the gods they may grant your wishes. Ibn Fadlan saw Viking traders doing this.

A small bronze figure of the god Frey, found in Sweden. He wears a pointed cap, and is seated cross-legged, and tugs at his beard.

This little figure of a woman holding a drinking horn may represent a Valkyrie, a fierce female spirit. It is probably an amulet.

A figure of Odin from a Vendel helmet (from earlier Viking times). He is shown as a warrior accompanied by an eagle and a raven.

The metal-worker who used this soapstone mould wanted to be sure of customers. It casts both crosses and Thor's hammer.

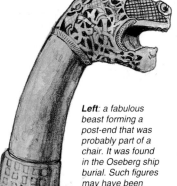

Left: a fabulous beast forming a post-end that was probably part of a chair. It was found in the Oseberg ship burial. Such figures may have been meant to frighten off evil spirits.

Warriors in the carving below seem to be making an offering to Odin. Three triangles are his symbol.

Left: amulet in the form of Thor's hammer.

Greenland's first church, built by the wife of Eric the Red.

THE COMING OF CHRISTIANITY

The first missionaries were allowed to build churches, but their bell-ringing was not popular.

If you decide to be baptised, you will be given new clothes, the symbol of a new life. Some people are baptised several times!

Harald Bluetooth, King of Denmark, is said to have been converted on seeing a bishop miraculously hold a bar of white-hot iron in his hand.

FIERCE FEMALE SPIRITS called Valkyries hover over the battlefield and take the slain to Asgard, where they are welcomed with horns full of ale.

THREE SISTERS WITH covered faces sit by a well beneath one of the roots of Yggdrasil. They are the Norns, the spirits who spin the thread of life and death.

Many stories are told of kindly but hot-tempered Thor. Once he went fishing and almost succeeded in catching the terrible world-serpent.

The mysterious god Odin gave the gift of poetry and the magic of runes to the world. He lost an eye in his search for wisdom.

The pagan gods were still remembered in Christian times, in stories told around the fireside, and in old songs the skalds sang. A skald was a professional poet kept by a Viking chief. His job was to entertain at feasts and to proclaim his employer's brave deeds in verse, so that they would never be forgotten. They tell of Odin's realm, Asgard, and of his eight-legged horse, Sleipnir, of Thor's mighty hammer, of the hero Sigurd the dragon-slayer, and many other tales.

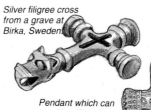

Silver filigree cross from a grave at Birka, Sweden.

Pendant which can be either Thor's hammer or a cross, according to which way up it is worn.

Frigg is the wife of Odin. She has a palace of her own where she sits spinning thread to weave into clouds.

The spiteful Loki often changes shape. When he was a mare he gave birth to Odin's eight-legged horse.

Baldur, whom all the gods loved, was killed by a shaft of mistletoe, through a trick of evil Loki.

Q

If you wanted to wash your clothes, why might a cow come in useful?
Go to page 21

If you were a slave where would you eat your meals?
Go to page 15

In the year 1000 Icelanders attending the Thing are ready to come to blows over whether or not the whole nation should become Christian.

The Lawspeaker lies in his tent all day and all night, considering. Then he urges the Vikings to be Christian and worship as they wish in private.

This satisfies everyone. Many are baptised at once, but some say the water is too cold. They want to wait till they reach their local hot springs.

YOUR HEALTH
HOW DO YOU KEEP CLEAN AND WELL?

The bathhouse is a separate stone-floored building with a drain, and a fire on which stones are heated.

When the stones are red hot, water is thrown on them filling the room with steam. Then you swelter in the heat.

If you like it very hot you can sit on the bench along the wall and whip yourself with a bundle of twigs.

This opens the pores and makes you sweat. To tone up you should then go outside and roll in the snow.

Q

You've decided to become a shipwright. How can you find out more about it?
Go to pages 28-29

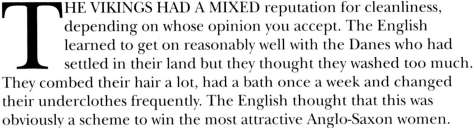

THE VIKINGS HAD A MIXED reputation for cleanliness, depending on whose opinion you accept. The English learned to get on reasonably well with the Danes who had settled in their land but they thought they washed too much. They combed their hair a lot, had a bath once a week and changed their underclothes frequently. The English thought that this was obviously a scheme to win the most attractive Anglo-Saxon women.

The Arab, Ibn Fadlan, who met the Vikings on the River Volga, formed a very different impression. They were as dirty as stray donkeys, he reported. They did not wash after going to the lavatory, or after a meal. Arabs were used to very high standards of cleanliness. Their civilisation was much more advanced than that of Europe, so there is no reason to think that the Vikings were less fussy than their neighbours. In fact, the Viking name for Saturday means bath day.

ABOVE IS the remains of a wooden lavatory seat found during the excavation of the Viking town at York. On the right is a suggestion of the sort of lavatory you might find it in. The seat goes over a hole in the ground or over a bucket. You may be the one who has to empty this.

Many Viking combs have been found. Women certainly needed them for their long hair, which was worn in a knot.

Travel could be dirty and tiring. Guests should be greeted with water, a towel and a hearty welcome.

They are given time to wash and refresh themselves, some dry clothes and a place by the fire.

The English disapproved of a Danish hairstyle that was very short at the neck and long in the fringe.

WASHING

An Arab travelling along the Volga described some Viking traders washing. He was disgusted by them.

He says that he saw a woman slave bring a bowl of water in which the first man washed his face and hair.

Then the man sneezed and blew his nose into the water before handing the bowl on to the next person.

The bowl was passed from man to man until each had washed his hair, and blown his nose in the same water.

An Arab travelling in Russia noticed that when Viking men needed to pee they went out in groups of four, with their hands on their swords, to protect each other.

Ibn Fadlan also thought poorly of Viking medical skills. This was not surprising, as Arab doctors were then the best in the world, apart from the Chinese. If you were wounded in battle you were bandaged and treated with herb poultices, but if these did not work people did not linger at your bedside. When Vikings saw that action was unlikely to get results they did not waste time on it. Illnesses were treated with traditional plant recipes but spells and amulets were also thought to be very effective. Runes were believed to have magical powers. They were carved on pieces of bone and put beneath a sick person's pillow and written on the palms of women in childbirth.

Studies of Viking skeletons show that many people suffered from wear and tear in the joints. They also prove that, as a Viking, your teeth will be worn to stumps by eating bread full of grit from the quern stones. However, this will not hurt, and your teeth will not decay because you do not eat sweets. There is no sugar!

A VIKING DIAGNOSIS

Your raiding party meets fierce resistance. An unexpected spear-thrust pierces your chest.

You are carried back to the camp where your wound is washed and you are given onion porridge to eat.

The porridge will help your companions to decide whether there is any hope of your getting better.

If they can smell onions through the wound they will know that the stomach has been pierced and you will die.

Combs with very fine teeth like this suggest that the Vikings might have found headlice a problem.

A scoop for cleaning the ears.

ICELANDERS HAVE extra encouragement to wash, as their land has volcanic hot springs. The hot-water bathing pool which Snorri Sturlson made at his farm at Reykholt is still there today.

TREATING THE SICK

The same Arab observer describes the way in which the Vikings he met treat someone who becomes ill.

They put the sick person in a tent by himself. This might have been a precaution against infection.

The invalid is left alone with some bread and water so that he has something to eat and drink if he feels strong enough.

Apart from this he gets hardly any attention. If he is a slave he is left entirely by himself.

If the sick man is lucky enough to recover he rejoins his companions. If he dies his body is burnt.

A slave is not thought to be worth burning. His body is left in the open to be eaten by dogs or vultures.

Q

Do you know where slaves come from? *Go to page 30-31*

Everybody is talking about the Thing. What is it? *Go to page 33*

FROM CRADLE TO GRAVE
BIRTH, MARRIAGE AND DEATH

Your mother is looked after by the women of the house. They wash you and take you to your father.

You are a strong healthy baby and he is delighted. He sprinkles you with water and gives you a name.

This means that he accepts you into the family. But if you are sickly he may not think you are worth rearing.

If so he may tell a servant to leave you in some exposed place where you will not survive long.

BIRTHS WERE always welcomed in a Viking family. Young people guaranteed the family's future survival. Vikings celebrated births and weddings with feasting and much ale drinking. Old age was not a time of life to be celebrated. In a cold climate, where hard work was needed to make crops grow and animals thrive, frail old people were a burden to their families. Though not actively cruel to the old, the Vikings did not regard them as a blessing. Women who survived the dangers of childbirth could live to over fifty. Men faced many perils and did not expect to live so long.

An ordinary person's grave. The body is placed directly in the earth in a wood-lined pit.

Horses slaughtered

Q

If someone insulted your family, what could you do about it?

Go to page 32

YOUR DEATH

Above: the funeral of a Viking chief, one of the leaders of the Viking traders in Russia. It was watched by an Arab traveller on the Volga in 922. This is what he tells his fellow travellers.

One of the dead man's slave-women must volunteer to die with him.

For ten days she is waited on by two attendants. She drinks and sings.

The chief lies in a temporary grave while special clothes are made for him.

On the day of the funeral his boat is hauled ashore onto a pile of wood.

A tent is set up on the boat, and it is spread with rugs and cushions.

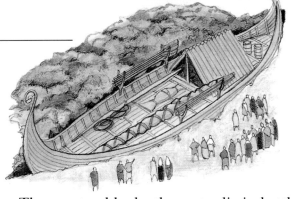

Left: this large ship burial must be for a rich man's funeral. A less important person might be buried in a small boat, or a boat-shaped grave marked by stones.

Below: the chief's followers set light to the ship. An old woman known as the Angel of Death carries away the dagger with which she has killed the slave.

YOU ARE MARRIED

The groom pays a 'bride-price' to his wife. He gets her dowry, but must return it if she leaves him.

The most noble death was to die in battle. A "straw death", which meant dying of old age on your mattress, was despised. Those who died on the battlefield joined Odin, the god of warriors, in his hall, Valhalla. Their bodies were either burnt or buried, according to the custom of their region. The objects that they needed in the afterlife were placed beside them. Women joined Frigg in her hall.

If you were the slave of a rich master or mistress you might have been chosen to die with them, an honour which it was difficult to refuse. However this was not a custom followed by all Vikings and was certainly not practised by Vikings who were Christians.

The couple join hands and drink bridal ale before witnesses, who must lead the man to his wife's bed.

If you are not happy with your husband you can get a divorce by declaring the fact before witnesses.

A dissatisfied husband can do the same. He can treat his women servants and slaves as wives.

Angel of death

The corpse is dug up, dressed in splendid clothes and put in the tent.

Two horses, two cows, a dog, a cock and a hen are killed and put with him.

The slave is lifted to look over a frame. She says she sees Paradise beyond.

She is led onto the ship, drinks a strong beverage and sings farewell, and is killed.

The ship is set ablaze. The nearest kinsman starts the fire.

A post bearing the dead man's name is set on the mound covering his ashes.

Q You have to feed your family. How can you bake some bread?
Go to page 18

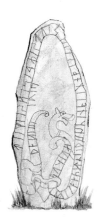

This Swedish rune stone records that Ulv from Uppland went raiding three times in England, and got a share in the silver taken.

A lion, now in Venice, received Viking graffiti when at its former site near Athens.

TO HELP US FIND out about the Vikings we have, first of all, their own messages to us on over 2,700 rune stones. These were put up to commemorate Viking people and their deeds. There are also the writings of people who lived at the time when the Vikings were active. Christian monks and Arab travellers have left vivid accounts of the Vikings as raiders and traders. Christian histories of the lives of kings and churchmen often refer to Viking lands. The Icelandic sagas, written more than two centuries after Viking times, have much to tell, though their picture of daily life in what was by then a bygone age may not be entirely accurate.

ALFRED THE GREAT, King of Wessex in England, recorded that a Norwegian chieftain called Ohthere visited his court in 890. He came from the far north where the Lapps of Lapland paid him tribute of furs, reindeer hides, walrus ivory and ropes made of skin.

THE VIKING FUNERAL described on pages 40 and 41 was witnessed on the river Volga by an Arab whose name was Ibn Fadlan.

He was acting as ambassador for the caliph of Baghdad. An account of his journey appears in an Arab book of geography.

Adam of Bremen, a German monk, wrote a history of the archbishops of Hamburg, in about 1075. It has much to tell about Viking lands and way of life.

The sagas, first written down in the 13th century, are traditional stories of Viking kings and heroes. Many were collected by the scholar Snorri Sturluson.

Archaeologists have found traces of Viking towns, farmsteads and burial sites. Objects of metal, glass and ceramics, which last well in the ground, show us the weapons, jewellery and tools people used. Human bones may reveal the diseases people had, how long they lived, and how they died.

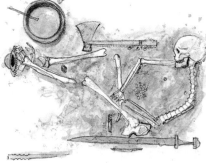

A man's grave discovered at Birka in Sweden. The objects buried with him included his sword, axe and spear, and a bronze dish.

The pagan custom of providing a corpse with valued possessions, food and tools to use in the afterlife has given us much information.

HOW DO WE KNOW?

The excavation of the Oseberg ship. The objects it contained had been preserved by airtight conditions within the mound. Lengthy exposure to air causes wood to decay. Contrary to what you might expect, water also preserves it. Sunken ships and remains found in water-logged sites (Hedeby for instance) have lasted well.

SCIENTIFIC analysis of refuse tells us about hygiene and diet, and timber may help to date a site through a process called dendro-chronology. The yearly rings of growth in trees vary in width, and wood of the same age shows the same variation. Timber can be dated if its rings match those in wood of a known date.

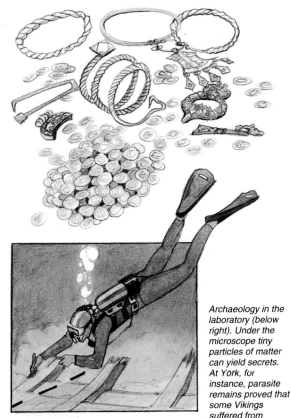

The Oseberg ship was old when it was buried. It can be dated by the style of the carving on its stem and stern post.

The burial was lavish, including beds and bedding, kitchen things, looms, a cart and four sledges, three splendidly carved.

The Oseberg burial mound had originally been 6 metres high and over 36 metres across. The ship was moored to a large stone within it. The corpses had been placed in a grave-chamber in the stern.
Archaeologists have established that the burial dates from the second half of the 9th century. Plant traces prove that it took place in August or September.

Below: Arab coins, found in hoards of Viking silver buried for safe-keeping, show the extent of trade with the south.

Goods buried with the Vikings give clues about their religious beliefs. Amongst the most spectacular Viking finds are two boat burials discovered in Norway, one at Gokstad in 1880 and the other at Oseberg in 1903. Previously it had been assumed the Viking ships were quite clumsily built. These vessels, both over 21 metres long, transformed people's knowledge of Viking skills.

The Oseberg ship, built around 800, seems to have been a pleasure boat made for shallow waters. A young woman had been buried in it, together with an elderly attendant and a host of objects that they might have needed.

The Gokstad ship, of about 850, was a more strongly built boat. It contained the bones of a man, twelve horses, six dogs and a peacock, as well as many personal objects and three rowing boats. A copy was built and it sailed successfully to America in 1893. Parts of the Viking towns hidden under modern York and Dublin have been excavated recently, and an entire village has been uncovered at Vorbasse in Denmark.

Replicas of ships have been tried out at sea to test speed, steering and rigging.

Diving to examine the wrecks of five Viking boats found in Roskilde fjord in Denmark. They were located in 1957.

The boats had been deliberately sunk to make a barrier across the fjord. One was a longship 28 metres in length.

Archaeology in the laboratory (below right). Under the microscope tiny particles of matter can yield secrets. At York, for instance, parasite remains proved that some Vikings suffered from intestinal worms.

The Vikings have left us few portraits. This head from Sweden shows a trimly bearded warrior.

TIMESPAN

AT THE DAWN OF THE VIKING age there were three great powers in the western world: the Franks who ruled what is now France and Germany, the Byzantines who had inherited the eastern half of the Roman Empire, and the Arabs whose civilisation extended from western Asia, through North Africa to Spain. Most of Europe, including Britain and Ireland, was Christian by this time, though the Scandinavians and the Slavs of eastern Europe were still pagan.

The Scandinavians were already prosperous traders in the areas around the Baltic sea. Before 700 the Swedes had expanded east-wards, setting up colonies along the Baltic coast. At the end of the 8th century the Norwegians made the first of what were to be repeated Viking attacks on countries to the west. No one knows for certain what caused these attacks, but it was probably a combination of greed for riches, and the need to find new land, as rising population created a shortage at home. Some settlers may have had a political motive in not wanting to submit to increasingly powerful kings.

793 Norwegian Vikings attack and destroy the monastery on the island of Lindisfarne which is off the Northumbrian coast of England. England at this time is divided into several small kingdoms of which Mercia, Wessex, East Anglia and Northumbria are the most important. There is no royal authority that is strong enough to organise a successful defence against these attacks.

795 They attack St. Columba's monastery at Iona in western Scotland, and raid the coast of Wales. c. 800 Norwegian Vikings land in the Orkney and Shetland Isles, and the Faroes. These provide a base for raids on Ireland.

810 King Godfred of Denmark invades neighbouring Frisia.

828 Irish chroniclers record that their country is overrun by Viking pirates.

834 Danes attack and raid the Frisian trading centre at Dorestad on the Rhine, and begin to launch regular attacks on the lands of the Franks.

835 The Danes attack Sheppey, an island at the mouth of the Thames, in England.

841 Norwegian Vikings begin to settle permanently in Ireland, and Dublin is founded. Ireland serves as a starting-point for the colonisation of the Isle of Man, south-western Scotland, and north-western England. In the same year the Danes sail up the Seine and attack and raid Rouen.

843 The Danes sail up the Loire River in France and attack Nantes. They destroy towns and monasteries all over western France. The terrified peasants flee, and the land is laid waste.

844 Vikings capture Seville in Spain, but only manage to hold it for a week as the Arabs soon put them to flight.

845 Paris in France, and Hamburg in Germany are attacked and plundered. Charles the Bald, who is king of the West Franks, pays the first of many large payments, known as Danegeld. This was used by the rulers to try to buy off the Vikings and stop their attacks.

850 Danes begin to overwinter in England.

859 A fleet of ships enters the Mediterranean where the Vikings raid for three years, overwintering on an island in the Rhone. They attack Spain, southern France, North Africa and Italy. They sack Pisa.

860-874 The first settlers arrive in Iceland.

864 Charles the Bald forbids the sale of weapons or horses to the Vikings.

865 A large Viking force lands in England seeking land to settle.

866 It captures York. By the early 870s Vikings control most of eastern England. They begin to share out the land. A further expansion is defeated by Alfred, King of Wessex, who makes its leaders accept Christianity.

886 A treaty between Alfred and Guthrum defines the frontier of the Danelaw. Alfred's successors gradually regain control in England though the Viking settlers remain.

891 Vikings are defeated by the Franks. Frankish defences are well organised and the Viking threat grows weaker on the continent.

911 Rollo is given Normandy by King Charles the Simple in exchange for a promise to defend France from other Vikings. Throughout the 10th century Swedish Vikings are active along trade routes in Russia.

c.960 Harald Bluetooth, King of Denmark, converts his country to Christianity.

980 A new wave of Viking attacks and raids on England begins.

c.986 Eric the Red goes to Greenland.

991 The English pay the first in a new series of Danegeld.

992 Leif Ericsson leaves Greenland to look for land to the west.

994 A fleet of 94 ships, led by Olaf Tryggvason of Norway and Svein Forkbeard of Denmark, attacks London.

995 Olaf, the Christian King of Norway, makes his people convert.

1009 Chief Thorkel the Tall, ravages England for three years and extorts 48,000 pounds of silver.

1013 Svein returns, and by 1017 controls all of England. His son Cnut rules until 1035. Cnut gains control of Norway and Sweden, and is also ruler of Denmark.

1042 The accession of an English king, Edward the Confessor, ends Danish rule in England.

1066 The Norwegian king Harald Hardraada invades England and is killed in battle at Stamford Bridge, near York. He is the last great Viking ruler.

c.1100 Close of the Viking age as Viking settlers become absorbed into the local populations.

1406-10 Icelanders visiting Greenland report back that Viking descendants are still to be found there. By the 16th century only the native Inuit people remain.

Q1 If you heard that someone had lost half his quern would you think he was having difficulty

A thinking straight?
B making bread?
C finding his way at sea?

Q2 Thor is the name of

A the season when the snows melt?
B the thunder god?
C the town founded by Godfred of Denmark?

Q3 Greenland is so called because its

A discoverers thought it needed an attractive name?
B its snow looks greenish in the distance?
C it was discovered by Erik the Green?

Q4 Your knorr is over-loaded. Is it likely to

A capsize?
B refuse to go at more than a walking pace?
C reveal what a greedy eater you are?

Q5 The Norns are

A three dangerous rocks off the Orkneys?
B three mysterious women?
C three giants?

Q6 Bjarni is the name of

A the god who was killed by a shaft of mistletoe?
B the man who missed the chance to be the first European in America?
C the bishop who converted Harald Bluetooth?

Q7 Sleipner is the name of

A Odin's horse?
B Thor's hammer?
C the world-serpent?

Q8 Skraeling is the Viking term for

A a person you think is a savage?
B a coarse cloth you think is only fit for slaves?
C a wad of animal hair used in caulking boats?

Q9 Tablet weaving is

A an interwoven pattern found only on rune stones?
B a way of making checked cloth?
C a way of making patterned ribbon?

Q10 Cnut was

A the discoverer of Iceland?
B the King of England?
C the man killed by Eric the Red?

Q11 Vikings remember Sigurd because he killed

A a famous dragon?
B a famous missionary?
C a Frankish king?

Q12 You have been spending time at the sheiling. Have you been

A steering a boat?
B judging a family dispute?
C grazing cattle?

Q13 Soapstone is

A a large rock near a river on which clothes are scrubbed?
B a soft rock from which bowls are carved?
C a semi-precious stone used by beadmakers?

Q14 Dendro-chronology is

A the method used to assess the probable speed of Viking boats?
B the term for an early way of telling the time?
C a technique for dating objects made of wood?

Q15 A skald is

A a Viking entertainer?
B a Viking dagger?
C a Viking drinking toast?

TO FIND OUT what your survival rating is *go to page 48.*

GLOSSARY

AMULET a small object, either worn or carried, which was thought to ward off evil.

BOG-IRON lumps of iron ore which are found in marshy ground.

BYRE a cow house.

CAULKING tarred animal hair put between the side planking of a boat to make it watertight.

CLEATS small pieces of wood fastened to, or left projecting from, the timbers of a ship.

CALIPH the title given to the supreme ruler of the Moslems.

COPPICE to cut back young shrubs or trees regularly, so that they form thickets of slender stems.

CORNELIAN a reddish semi-precious stone.

DAMASCENING the process of fusing iron and steel to produce a wavy pattern.

DAUB a mixture of mud and straw.

DISTAFF a long cleft stick on which a spinner holds the wool or flax about to be spun.

FILIGREE an openwork decoration on jewellery, made of gold or silver wire and tiny balls of gold or silver.

GRIDDLE a metal support with a handle, used for cooking bread, cakes, etc., over a fire.

GROUND-WATER water that collects naturally some distance below ground.

KEEL the lowest lengthwise timber of a boat, on which the sides are built up.

MAGNETIC behaving as a magnet. The earth is a magnet. Its poles will attract a magnetised compass needle.

MISSIONARY a Christian sent to another country to convert its people to Christianity.

PAGAN belonging to a faith that is not Christian.

ROVE a small metal plate over which the protruding end of a nail is bent and hammered flat.

RUNES Viking alphabet. Letters used for casting spells and writing.

SADDLERY saddles and other leather equipment for horses.

STARBOARD the right-hand side of a boat.

STAVE a thin, narrow piece of wood.

VALHALLA the Viking heaven.

VALKYRIES Odin's nine daughters, and fierce female spirits of Viking legend.

VENDEL belonging to Scandinavian culture of the two centuries before the Viking age, named after finds made at Vendel, Sweden.

VENISON deer meat.

WARP THREADS threads which run lengthwise in woven material. In an upright loom they hang down. Weft threads are woven across them.

YEASTS microscopic fungi, often used for baking bread.

ANSWERS

HAVE YOU SURVIVED?

Here are the quiz answers, with pages to turn to if you need an explanation.

Q

1 (B) - page 18	8 (A) - page 35
2 (B) - page 36	9 (C) - page 26
3 (A) - page 33	10 (B) - page 45
4 (A) - page 29	11 (A) - page 37
5 (B) - page 37	12 (C) - page 22
6 (B) - page 35	13 (B) - page 27
7 (A) - page 37	14 (C) - page 43
	15 (A) - page 37

Count up your correct answers and find out what your survival rating is.

14 - 15 Excellent! You could be a Viking chief.
11 - 13 You would make a good loyal follower of the chief.
6 - 10 You might do better to stay at home by the fire.
5 - 0 Terrible! You would be sold as a slave!

ACKNOWLEDGEMENTS
The Salariya Book Co Ltd would like to thank the following people for their assistance:

Sarah Ridley
Penny Clarke
Jenny Millington

PRINTED IN BELGIUM BY
proost
INTERNATIONAL BOOK PRODUCTION

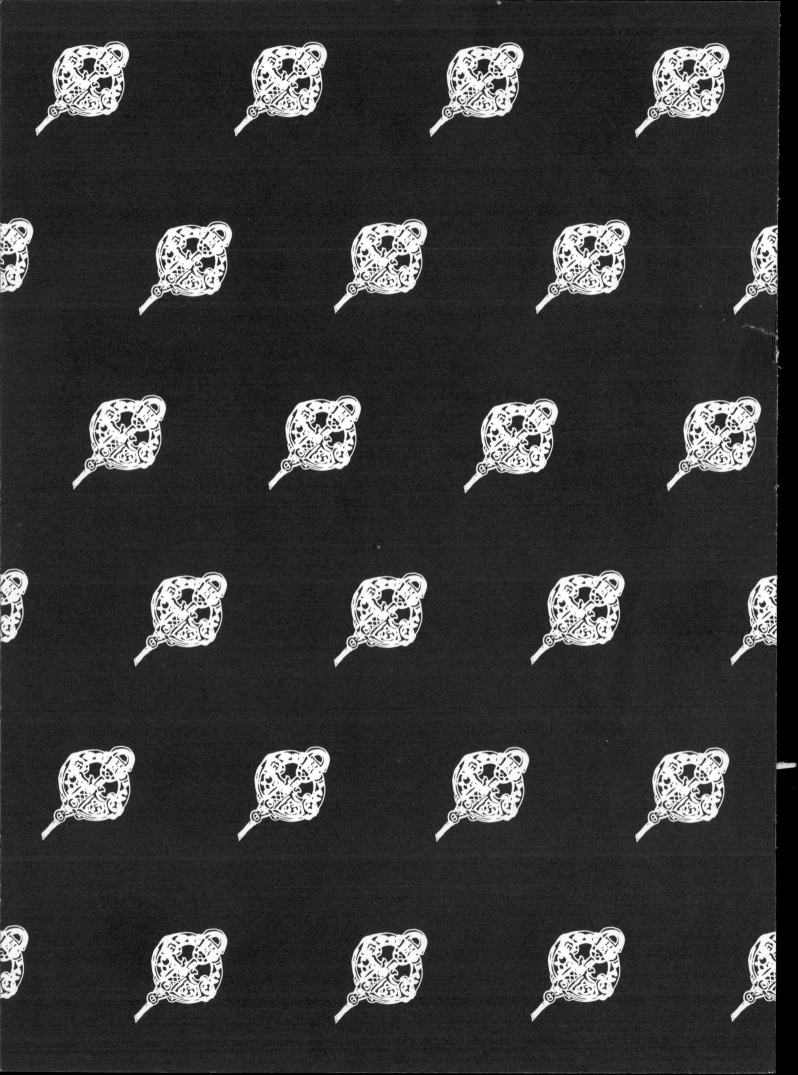